HOBBIES FOR EVERYONE...

An Introduction to RADIO-CONTROLLED SAILPLANES

Written and photographed
by Tony Freeman

Consultant, Dan Pruss,
Captain, North Central Airlines

 CHILDRENS PRESS, CHICAGO

Library of Congress Cataloging in Publication Data

Freeman, Tony.
  Radio-controlled sailplanes.

  (Hobbies for everyone)
  SUMMARY: A brief introduction to the equipment
and techniques necessary to the operation of radio-
controlled model sailplanes.
  1. Gliders (Aeronautics)—Models—Radio control
—Juvenile literature. [1. Gliders (Aeronautics)—
Models—Radio control] I. Title. II. Series.
TL770.F715   629.133'1'32   78-12719
ISBN 0-516-03570-3

Since people first looked into the sky, they have wanted to be able to join the birds and FLY!

Today the aircraft that most closely resembles a bird in flight is the sailplane. This lightweight plane has no engine. It is usually towed into the air by an airplane. Once it is high enough it releases its tow line. Sailplanes ride on rising warm air currents, called *thermals*. With good thermals a sailplane can stay aloft for hours.

Sailplanes are fun to fly. But not everyone who wants to fly can afford to. For these people, the answer is a RC (radio-controlled) model sailplane.

These planes gained popularity in the United States about 1965. It is estimated that there are now more than 10,000 radio-controlled sailplane pilots in the United States.

The planes come apart for carrying to and from the flying area.

All the tools and parts a pilot might need in the field can be carried in a small box such as this one.

The sport of model sailplane flying has become so popular that prices on planes and radios are not as expensive as they once were. A model plane kit now costs about as much as a good basketball. The radio-control units can be purchased for less than the price of a ten-speed bike.

The planes are quite large. Some of them have wings that are longer than a car. However, they are very light. They seldom weigh more than three pounds including the radio equipment in the plane.

Sailplanes usually have long wingspans in order to take advantage of the rising air currents. *Wingspan* means how long the wing is from tip to tip. Wingspans range from six feet to over 12 feet.

Wings can have several types of shapes. The "V" shaped wing is called *dihedral*. An extra "V" out toward the tips—as in the picture above—is called *polyhedral*. Dihedral and polyhedral angles make the sailplane more stable when being flown.

Most radio-controlled sailplanes use only two channels. One of them makes the plane go up and down. The other makes it turn right or left. The radio does this by making little motors called *servos* operate inside the plane. The little black box in the nose of this plane is the radio receiver. It tells the two servos right behind it in the compartment when to work. This is very much like the garage door openers some people have in their cars.

The control stick on the radio-control unit operates just as it would in a real airplane. If the pilot pulls back on the stick, the plane will go up.

If he pushes forward on the stick, the plane will go down.

A push to the left makes the plane turn to the left.

Pushing the stick to the right causes the plane to turn right.

The model sailplanes can be launched into the air by an electric winch powered by a car battery. This is similar to a big fishing reel. It has a long cord that rolls up on a drum. The plane is pulled by the cord and flies with this power up to about 300 feet in the air.

To launch a sailplane, the pilot slips the end of the launch cord over a small hook built into the plane. When the plane gets very high, the loop slips off the hook and floats to the ground on a parachute. The aircraft then flies as long as the pilot can find thermals.

When the foot switch of the winch is operated, the plane flies into the sky as it is released.

Another way to put a sailplane into the air is with a giant rubber band called a high-start.

Some sailplanes have landing skids. Others don't. Skids help to stop the model after it lands. Sometimes the flier catches the model in midair.

It takes about six months to be able to fly very well and even pilots who have been flying for years are always working to improve. No one feels he is as good as he can get.

These pilots are all members of a sailplane club and are flying in a safe place selected by the club. The first thing a new flier should do is join such a club. This way he can learn from the more experienced pilots.

Part of the fun of flying with a club is being with friends who share your interest in model sailplanes.

New members get a lot of help from older members. This club member helps a novice unwind the launching winch. Some clubs even have flight training programs to teach beginners.

Youngsters who don't fly can help by running the stopwatch to time flights. Club members are as young as eight years old. Younger members usually start by building non-flying models until they learn to fly the big ones.

Most clubs are members of the AMA (Academy of Model Aeronautics) which helps them with contests, a magazine, insurance, and other aids. The members often admire each other's workmanship on the models. Careful work pays off with pats on the back and good flights.

By working together as a club, pilots can get more cooperation
from park departments and city councils to reserve flight areas.

Usually hobby shop discounts on planes like these are offered to club members. This can save more money each year than the dues would cost.

Club members always fly in an authorized safety area. Other members can give the pilot a hand if his plane lands on a roof or in a tree.

Clubs have monthly meetings with guest speakers and other programs. They also hold flight sessions and contests each week.

Families enjoy this hobby together. Anyone can learn to fly, especially if others help.

Some club members compete in many different contests. There are speed races. In these races specially designed sailplanes can reach 90 miles per hour. The normal speed is about 20 miles per hour.

Clubs often meet to see how long they can keep their planes in the air. If the air is good, they can fly for hours!

Another contest requires the pilot to land as close to a target as possible in exactly two minutes. When the plane lands, the pilot can tip it forward onto skids glued under the plane's nose to brake it to a stop.

Many model sailplane pilots belong to an organization called the League of Silent Flight (LSF). Pilots earn ratings in the league by improving their flying. They have to be able to land close to a target, fly for certain times, and win contests. There are five levels. Level one is easy to reach, but level five is so hard that only a few league members have done it. Most hobby shops can tell you how to get in touch with either the LSF or the Academy of Model Aeronautics. They will send you the addresses of clubs near you.

Friends in a club will usually help a new member build his plane. It is a lot easier to do with guidance from experienced builders.

A table at least as large as the plans that come with the plane kit will be needed to assemble the model. The builder needs to be able to pin parts of the plane in place while the glue dries. The top of the table should be a bulletin board kind of material.

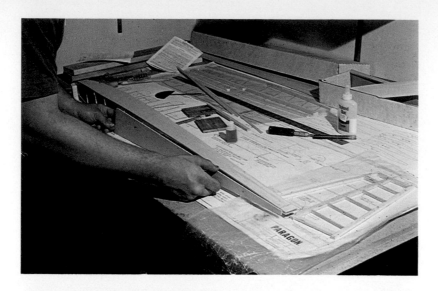

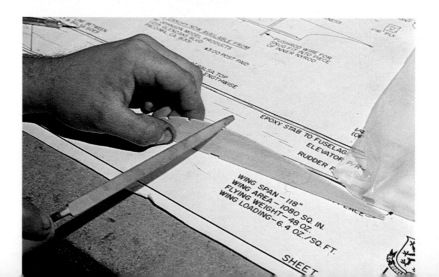

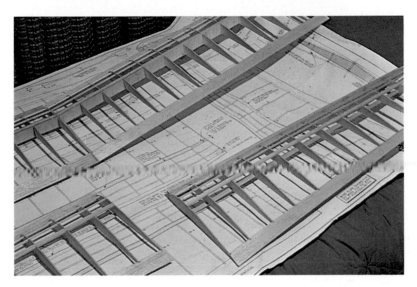

Usually all parts needed to build the plane come in the kit except the wing covering and the radio gear.

Building the models is not much different than building any "stick" models except that all the parts are larger and easier to handle. A miniature saw will be needed to cut some of the long sticks. Other parts are pre cut but need a little sanding to fit into place.

It takes 50 to 100 hours of work to build a model and cover it.

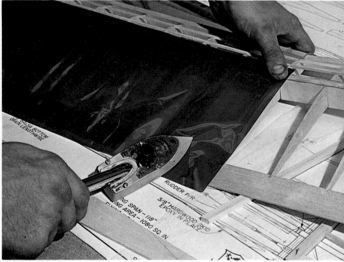

The wing covering is a very strong plastic. It is attached to the wing and held in place by melting it onto the wooden parts of the wing with a small electric iron. The heat also shrinks the material, leaving the surface very smooth.

The wings are usually built in two parts. They are hooked together and fastened to the *fuselage* (the body of the plane) with strong rubber bands. Assembly is done at the flying field.

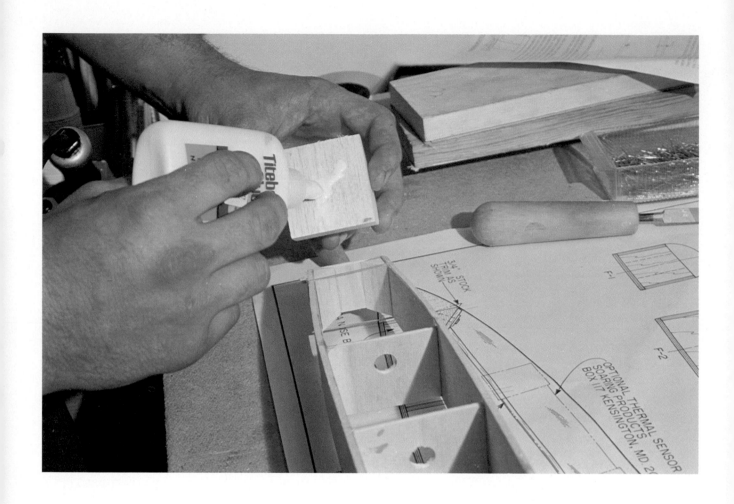

Different kinds of glue are used at various places on the plane. Household white glue and epoxy glue provide great strength. The new "space-age" glue works very quickly.

Builders of model planes can buy items such as this servo in hobby shops where they can also get a lot of help with their model building.

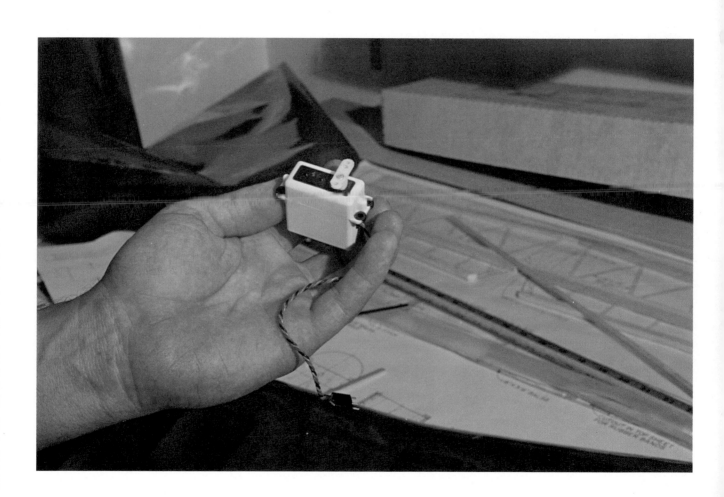

This champion flier builds his planes with great care and has many trophies to show as a result. Model aviation can lead to many kinds of careers including engineering, commercial flying, and military flying.

Many pilots like to fly their homemade radio-controlled sailplanes from a hillside. This is called *slope* flying. A wind usually blows on the side of a hill and the plane is launched by simply throwing the plane into the wind by hand.

The pilot holds the radio-control unit in one hand.

He throws the plane into the breeze.

The breeze up the slope keeps the plane airborne.

Once the plane is airborne, the pilot has great control over the sailplane to keep it aloft.

The flight can be quite remarkable. Some fliers have recorded flights of over eight hours on the slopes!

With the hand-held transmitter, the pilot can control the plane for as far as it can be seen. Having your name and phone number on the plane is a good idea, in case you do fly it out of sight. Many once-lost models have been returned.

Sometimes the wind on the slope dies and the plane lands wherever it wants to. When this happens, it helps to be a good hiker.

Those who fly model sailplanes are operating the same controls a real pilot would. They are standing on the ground instead of riding inside the plane. Most pilots of model sailplanes try to imagine that they are inside their planes because it is easier to fly that way. And more fun.

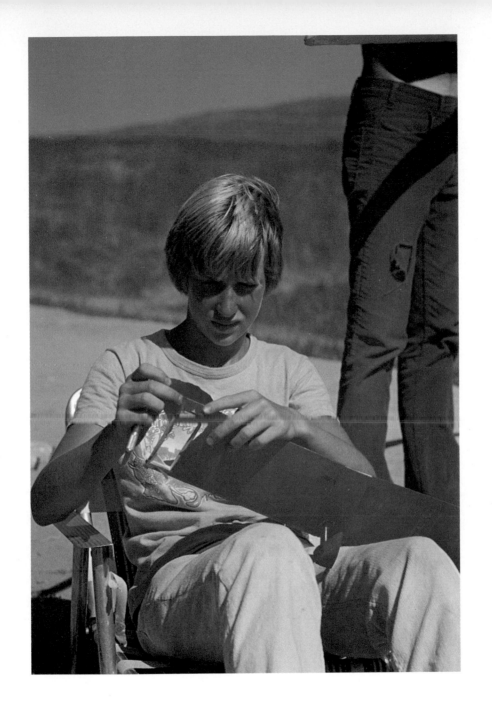

Pilots expect to have to do a certain amount of repair work now and then. Minor repairs are usually made at the flying field.

More people are building and flying sailplanes all the time.
They like soaring because it is quiet, less expensive than some
other sports, and more challenging.

About the Author/Photographer

Tony Freeman has taught photography at Anaheim High School in Anaheim, California since 1962. He feels that a teacher should be active in the field he is teaching. For this reason, as well as to help feed his wife and six children, he has provided several thousand photographs to publications across the nation as a freelance photographer for the last fifteen years.

He began writing a few years ago when several magazines asked for words with his photographs, and has since become a busy writer-photographer.

Freeman has been active with his children in Boy and Girl Scouting, school bands, and church activities. He is around young people so much that he considers himself a child at heart. So it was only natural that he turn to writing and illustrating children's books. He gets great pleasure from learning new things and sharing these discoveries with young people, both in his classroom and in his books.